Historical Letters, Diaries and Jo

selected by J

Contents

The Paston Letters

John Paston often had to go to London, while his wife managed their estates in Norfolk. Theirs are the earliest family letters known in English.

Margaret Paston to John Paston I

1448

Right worshipful husband, I recommend me to you, and pray you to get some crossbows, and windases[1] to bend them with, and quarrels[2];

[1] machinery for winding crossbows back – longbows could be pulled by hand, but crossbows were too strong

[2] special short arrows for crossbows

for your houses here been so low that there may none man shoot out with no long bow, though we had never so much need ... And also I would ye should get two or three short poleaxes[1] to keep with doors, and as many jacks[2], an ye may ...

I pray you that ye will vouchsafe[3] to don buy for me 1lb of almonds and 1lb of sugar, and that ye will do buyen some frieze[4] to maken of your childer's gowns.

[1] a kind of axe used as a weapon
[2] footsoldiers' sleeveless, padded leather tunics
[3] be kind enough to
[4] a coarse woollen cloth

Ye shall have best cheap and best choice of Hay's wife, as it is told me. And that ye would buy a yard of broadcloth of black for an hood for me, of 44d or 4s a yard, for there is neither good cloth nor good frieze in this town. As for the childer's gowns, an I have cloth I shall do them maken.

The Trinity have you in his keeping and send you good speed in all your matters.

Shakespeare and the Elizabethan Theatre

Shakespeare left no diaries or letters, but other people have recorded seeing his plays. Thomas Platter of Basle wrote a journal of his trip to England, including his visits to the theatre.

Portrait of William Shakespeare by Ford Madox Brown.

September 21st 1599

After dinner, at about two o'clock, I went with my party across the river; in the straw-thatched house we saw the tragedy of the first Emperor Julius Caesar, very pleasantly performed, with approximately fifteen characters; at the end of the play they danced together admirably and exceedingly gracefully, according to their custom, two in each group dressed in men's and two in women's apparel[1].

[1] clothing

A letter from Sir Henry Wotton to his nephew, describes the burning down of the first Globe Theatre.

2nd June 1613

The King's players had a new play ... representing some principal pieces of the reign of Henry VIII ... Now, King Henry making a masque[1] at the Cardinal Wolsey's house, and certain chambers[2] being shot off at his entry, some of the paper ... wherewith one of them was stopped[3], did light on the thatch, where being thought at first but an idle smoke, and their eyes more attentive to the show, it kindled

---

[1] a kind of play

[2] guns

[3] stuffed into the barrel to make a flash and smoke

8 *Replica of the Globe Theatre and actors performing Shakespeare's Merchant of Venice.*

inwardly, and ran round like a train[1], consuming within less than an hour the whole house to the very grounds.

... yet nothing did perish but wood and straw, and a few forsaken cloaks; only one man had his breeches set on fire, that would perhaps have broiled[2] him, if he had not by the benefit of a provident wit[3], put it out with bottle ale.

---

[1] a long fuse for gunpowder, like a touch-paper on a firework

[2] burned

[3] quick thinking

Samuel Pepys and the Great Plague of 1665

Samuel Pepys (1633-1703) kept a diary between 1660 and 1669.

July 13th 1665: Above 700 died of the plague this week.

30th: It was a sad noise to hear our bell to toll and ring so often today, either for death or burials.

August 10th: By and by to the office ... in great trouble to see the Bill[1] this week rise so high ... above 3000 of the plague.

[1] the Bill of Mortality, published every week, listed how many people had died in each parish

12th: The people die so, that now ... they... carry the dead to be buried by day-light, the nights not sufficing to do it in.

15th: I met a dead corpse of the plague, in the narrow alley ...

31st: In the City died this week ... 6102 of the plague.

September 3rd (Lord's day)

Alderman Hooper told us of a saddler, who had buried all the rest of his children of the plague, and himself and wife now being shut up and in despair of escaping, did desire only to save the life of his little child; and so prevailed to have it received stark-naked into the arms of a friend, who brought it (having put it into new fresh clothes) to Greenwich.

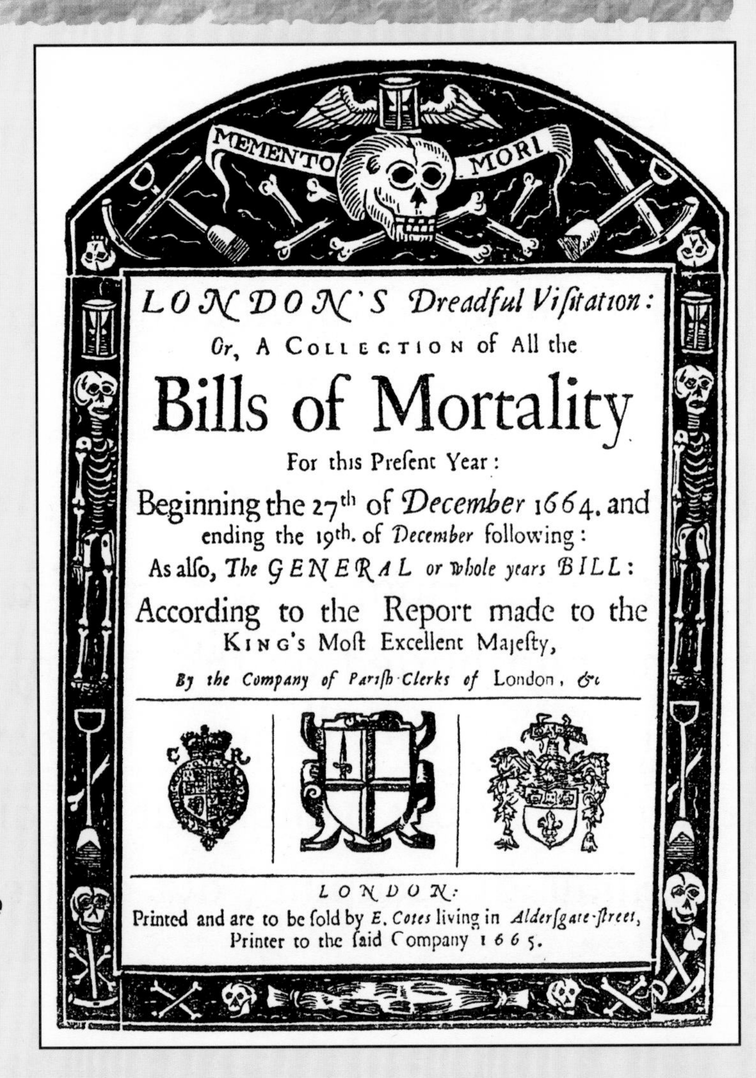

LONDON'S Dreadful Viſitation:

Or, A COLLECTION of All the

Bills of Mortality

For this Preſent Year:

Beginning the 27th of *December* 1664. and ending the 19th. of *December* following:

As alſo, *The GENERAL or whole years BILL:*

According to the Report made to the KING's Moſt Excellent Majeſty,

By the Company of Pariſh Clerks of London, &c

LONDON:

Printed and are to be ſold by *E. Cotes* living in *Alderſgate-ſtreet,* Printer to the ſaid Company 1665.

Bill of Mortality from the Great Plague of 1665.

John Evelyn and the Great Fire of London

John Evelyn (1620–1706) was a wealthy man who wrote several books and also kept a diary.

September 2 1666: This fatal night about ten, began that deplorable fire, neere Fish-streete ...

3: I saw the whole South part of the Citty burning ... there was nothing heard or seene but crying out & lamentation, & running about like distracted creatures ... Here we saw the Thames coverd with ... all the barges & boates laden with what some had time & courage to save ...

all the skie were of a fiery aspect, like the top of a burning Oven, & the light seene above 40 miles round about for many nights: God grant mine eyes may never behold the like, who now saw above ten thousand houses all in one flame, the noise & crakling & thunder of the impetuous flames, the

The Great Fire of London by Dutch School.

shreeking of Women & children, the hurry of people, the fall of towers, houses & churches was like an hideous storme, & the aire all about so hot & inflam'd that at the last one was not able to approch it ...The Clowds also of Smoke were dismall, & reached ... neere 50 miles in length.

4: The burning still rages ... but the courage of the multitude persisting, & innumerable houses blown up with Gunpowder, such gaps & desolations were soone made.

7: I went this morning on foote from White hall as far as London bridge ... with extraordinary difficulty, clambring over mountaines of yet smoking rubbish, & frequently mistaking where I was, the ground under my feete so hott, as made me not onely Sweate, but even burnt the soles of my shoes.

The Journal of Charlotte Brontë

Charlotte Brontë wrote this on 12 March 1829 when she was thirteen. She had only been to school for one year, when she was eight. She and her sisters and brother had their lessons at home with their aunt.

> Once papa lent my Sister Maria A Book it was an old Geography and she wrote on its Blank leaf papa lent me this Book. the Book is an hundred and twenty years old it is at this moment lying Before me while I write this I am in the kitchin of the parsonage house Haworth

Taby the servent is washing up after Breakfast and Anne my youngest Sister (Maria was my eldest[1]) is kneeling on a chair looking at some cakes whiche Tabby has been Baking for us. Emily is in the parlour brushing it papa and Branwell are gone to Keighly Aunt is up stairs in her Room and I am siting by the table writing this in the kitchin. Keighly is a small twon four miles from here   papa and Branwell are gone for the newspaper the Leeds Intelligencer ...

[1] Maria had died five years earlier

Queen Victoria's Diaries

In 1833, aged thirteen, Princess Victoria wrote about her day.

It was a *delightful ride*. We cantered a good deal. SWEET LITTLE ROSY went BEAUTIFULLY!! We came home at a $\frac{1}{4}$ past 1 ... At 20 minutes to 7 we went out to the Opera ... Rubini came on and sang a song out of "Anna Boulena" *quite beautifully*. We came home at $\frac{1}{2}$ past 11.

In 1835 she recorded first impressions of her cousins, Princes Ernest and Albert of Saxe-Coburg.

Ernest ... has dark hair, and fine dark eyes and eyebrows, but the nose and mouth are not good; he has a most kind, honest and intelligent expression in his countenance[1], and has a very good figure. Albert, who is just as tall as Ernest but stouter, is extremely handsome; his hair is about the

Prince Albert

[1] face

same colour as mine; his eyes are large and blue, and he has a beautiful nose and a very sweet mouth with fine teeth, but the charm of his countenance is his expression, which is most delightful ...

On 20 June 1837, Victoria became Queen. That night she wrote:

Since it has pleased Providence to place me in this station, I shall do my utmost to fulfil my duty towards my country; I am very young, and perhaps in many, though not in all things, inexperienced, but I am sure that very few have more real good will and more real desire to do what is fit and right than I have.

Queen Victoria in her coronation robes (1837) from the Jubilee Book of Queen Victoria.

The Wonderful Adventures of Mary Seacole

Mary Seacole was born in Jamaica. Her mother was a Jamaican traditional healer, and Mary became a skilful nurse. In 1854 she came to London and heard of the agonies suffered by sick and wounded soldiers in the Crimea. Despite being turned away by all the officials, she travelled to work there.

A journalist wrote in *The Times*:

> She is always in attendance near the battle-field to aid the wounded, and has earned many a poor fellow's blessing ... I have seen her go down under fire with her little store of creature comforts for our wounded men, and a more tender or skilful hand about a wound or a broken limb could not be found among our best surgeons.

After Mary Seacole returned to England her health was poor. A letter to *The Times* demanded:

> Sir,
>
> Where are the Crimeans? Have a few months erased from their memories those many acts of comforting kindness which made the name of the old mother venerated[1] throughout the camp? While the benevolent deeds of Florence Nightingale are being handed down to posterity[2] ... are the humbler actions of Mrs Seacole to be entirely forgotten?

In 1857 Mary wrote her memoirs, *The Wonderful Adventures of Mrs Seacole in Many Lands.*

---

[1] greatly respected

[2] remembered by people in the future

"Account of the Year 1864" by Hannah Cullwick, Servant

When this year began i was general servant to Mr Foster the beer merchant, at 22 Carlton Villas. i was kitchen servant like, & did all the dirty work down stairs, besides the dining room & hall & steps & back stairs. There were 12 steps to the front door, & it took me $\frac{1}{2}$ an hour to clean 'em crawling backwards ... i clean'd all the boots & knives & some o the windows & the grates belonging to the dining room, kitchen & the room down stairs what the children play'd in & the nurse sat in to work & that – i had 3 or 4 pair o boots of a day & about 2 dozen knives & six forks – & i clean'd the watercloset & privy & the passage & all the rough places down stairs & my wages was 15 lbs[1] a year.

[1] £15

A Letter From Beatrix Potter

Beatrix Potter often wrote to the children of her governess. Here she writes about celebrations for Queen Victoria's Diamond Jubilee.

June 14th 1897

My dear Frida,

... What a nice time you are having, going to so many tea parties. I wonder if there are going to be any decorations at Wandsworth on Jubilee Day. I shall not go to see the procession; it is too hot. I shall stop at home and hang a large flag out of the window.

Queen Victoria's Diamond Jubilee procession passes the National Gallery, Trafalgar Square (1897).

At the last Jubilee there was a wind, and our flag kept rolling up. We had to reach out of the window with a broom to unroll it. We are going to have nightlights on the window sills, red, blue and white.

My rabbit is so hot he does not know what to do with himself. He has such thick fur, I think he would be more comfortable if he had a little coat which would take off ... I remain

Yours affectionately

Beatrix Potter

Roald Dahl

Roald Dahl went to boarding school when he was nine. He wrote to his mother every week.

Dec 8th 1925

Dear Mama,

Just to make it a bit planer I will be coming home on December 17th, not the 18th. I will arrive a Cardiff a four o'clock please meet me, if that is not planer noufe let me know what you want to know about it.

Love from

Boy

In 1929 Roald went to Repton school. He wrote about his daily life there.

I don't think that I've told you what we do every day satisfactorily; the first bell goes at quarter past seven and the fag[1] who is on water in each bedder[2], gets up and fills the cans with hot water, and loses the windows. Then if he wants to go to bed again, the second bell goes at half past seven and everyone must be down for prayers by quarter to eight.

[1] younger boy who acted as the servant of an older boy in whose study (room) he had a desk
[2] dormitory

Artist's impression of life at a boarding school.

In 1939 Roald was working in Africa.

Dar es Salaam

5th June 1939

Dear Mama,

It's pleasant lying back and listening to and at the same time watching the antics of Hitler and Mussolini who are invariably on the ceiling catching flies and mosquitoes. Hitler and Mussolini are 2 lizards which live in our sitting room. They're always here, and apart from being very useful about the house they are exciting to watch. You can see Hitler (who is smaller than Musso and not so fat) fixing his unfortunate victim – often a small moth – with a very hypnotic eye ...

Letters From an Evacuee

Hilda Hollingsworth and her sister Pat, aged ten and seven, were evacuated to Wales in 1940. Hilda was often unhappy. At school, her class copied a letter from the blackboard:

Dear Mum (and Dad),

Thank you for your lovely letter (and pocket money) which (I) (we) (was) (were) very pleased to receive. It is very nice living here in the countryside. (Miss) (Mrs) _________ is a very kind lady and (I am) (we are) very happy with her. (I) (We) hope that you are all well and happy too. On Saturday ____________________.

With lots of love from your (daughter) (son)

(Ann Best) (John Brown)

Once when Hilda found a stamp, she wrote a secret letter to her mother:

Dear Mum,

I hope you are well and happy. Please can we come home. Pat and me are both in different homes. We're lonely, come and get us Mum, PLEASE.

Lots of love from your loving daughter
Hilda

Please don't tell no one I wrote.

Diary of an Air-raid

Colin Perry, aged eighteen, kept a diary from March to November 1940.

Sunday 18th August 1940

We had just settled down to a delightful dinner – chicken, marrow, peas, new potatoes and baked potatoes, stuffing and gravy, when the air-raid sirens started ... Aircraft were roaring overhead, and ... having deposited my belongings safely below ground ... I went across to No. 1 block to the top floor, and sure enough Croydon once again was in smoke ... As I was looking out I heard a terrific roar approaching, ... so I ran into the court, to the shelter, where everyone was busily scanning the sky. Then I shouted ... some 30 or 40 enemy bombers, accompanied by fighters, were sweeping in a direct line for Croydon. They were indeed very near us. It presented an amazing spectacle, like a swarm of bees surrounding their queen ... A puff of smoke and the sound of a gun signalled our retreat down the shelter. I fancied I heard the whine of dive-bombers, most assuredly we heard the guns and crunch of falling bombs.

Fellows only a year my senior are up there shooting the raiders down, and within a year I too hope to be there... The 'all clear' sounded soon after, and we went back to cold chicken. Damn, the only time for months we have had a chicken and then the Nazis have to spoil it.

The Most Important Lessons in Life

An American girl wrote this letter to 200 famous people:

> Hello, my name is Rachel Chandler. I live in Roanoke, Virginia. I am 11 years old, and I am in the 7th grade. I have a learning disability, but I work very hard and make the honor roll in school. My dad says that I can do or be anything if I work hard. He says that girls are as smart as boys. I may be a doctor or a writer when I grow up.
>
> What do you think is the most important thing to learn in life? My dad says that I should have determination and my mom says to

know the importance of family. I am writing to great people to get advice. I am writing a report for my Girl Scout project and for school.

Thank you for helping me.

Love
Rachel Chandler

This is one of the replies she received:

Dear Rachel,

I feel that I am a very lucky man to have the love and respect of such wonderful young people from all over the world.

I think the most important thing to learn in life is how to live with all sorts of people and to make each other happy and content. I think we must all strive to be at peace with ourselves and each other.

Your mum and dad are very lucky to have such a wonderful young daughter, and I am sure you are going to be a doctor or writer one day. Keep working hard and you will achieve.

I am deeply honoured that you wrote to me and I thank you.

With warm wishes to you and your family,

Yours sincerely

Nelson Mandela

Nelson Mandela President of South Africa (1994–99)

Nelson Mandela.